Most of the time, I like school. Mrs Simms, my teacher, is nice. Most of the children in my class are nice too.

I used to like mornings. That's when we do maths, my favourite subject.

But for the past few weeks, I've been having trouble concentrating.

The bell rings for lunch, and everyone leaves.
I stay in my seat, my stomach twisting in knots.

"Stevie?" Mrs Simms says when she sees I'm still there.
"Did you hear the bell?"

I hate lunchtime and don't want to go. But I say, **"Yes,"** and shuffle slowly down the corridor.

I hear footsteps behind me. I hold my breath.

"Hey, stupid." Jean shoves me in the back. **"You're late."**

I keep moving, hoping Jean will leave me alone.

Then one of Jean's friends steps in front of me, and I have to stop. I start to cry. I don't want to, but I'm scared.

Jean grabs hold of my arm and twists me around.

"What's wrong, baby?" Jean says. **"Do you want your mummy?"**

Physical bullying often happens in places that aren't closely supervised, such as toilets or corridors, or busy areas such as the school playground.

"Stop it!" I yell. **"Leave me alone!"** I try to pull away, but Jean punches me in the stomach and takes my lunch box.

I fall, gasping for breath and crying even louder.

I spend the rest of lunchtime alone on a bench.

Physical bullying can include hitting, pushing, kicking, tripping, slapping, spitting and hair pulling. It can include stealing and harming personal belongings. Threatening to hurt someone is also bullying.

By the time I get home, I haven't eaten all day. I grab an apple and some biscuits.

"Hey, save room for your dinner," Mum says. "Didn't you eat lunch?"

"No. I ... I lost my lunch box," I say.

During my bath I try to hide my arm from her.

That night Mum sits with me in my room. "Stevie," she says, "I see your arm is bruised. And this isn't the first time you've lost your lunch box. When I was your age, some children used to push me. Has that ever happened to you?"

I'm embarrassed. Will Mum blame me for being bullied? Will she believe me? And I don't want to tell tales. What if Jean finds out and things get worse?

But I really need help, so I tell her about Jean.

Mum listens. Then she asks me to describe what Jean has been doing. I answer as best I can. I tell her how Jean twisted my arm and took my lunch box.

Telling an adult about bullying is not telling tales. When you tell someone, you are trying to protect yourself or someone else. When you tell tales, you are trying to get someone else into trouble.

"I'm very glad you told me," Mum says. "Bullying is not OK, and it's not your fault. Tomorrow I'm going to talk to your teacher about making this better. I also know some things you can do right now that may help. Do you want to hear them?"

I nod.

Mum tells me that confident children aren't bullied as much as worried and unhappy children. She says that if I keep my head up, my shoulders back and my arms at my sides, I will look more sure of myself. She also tells me to try not to cry.

"I know you cry because you're scared, and you yell because you're angry. But that's just what Jean wants. It makes Jean feel powerful when you get upset."

Fighting back may seem like a good way to respond to physical bullying. But it can get the person who's bullied into as much trouble as the person who bullies. Fighting may make the bullying get even worse.

I'm not sure I can do what she's telling me.

"You're very clever, Stevie," Mum says. "I bet you have some ideas for keeping safe."

I think about how Jean picks on me when I'm alone. "I suppose I could walk along with other children. And try to stay near adults."

"Great ideas." She kisses me goodnight. "Remember that I love you, and I'm always on your side. You're my little hero."

"Like Mighty Raccoon?" I ask.

She smiles. "Better than Mighty Raccoon."

Looking someone in the eyes is one way to appear stronger. Some people find it easier to look at the bridge of someone's nose rather than directly into their eyes.

The next day at school, my stomach twists, and I already feel like crying. Can I do what Mum taught me?

Then I think about Mighty Raccoon, who's super-strong and always in control. I imagine I'm Mighty Raccoon and don't feel so scared.

When the bell rings at lunchtime, I jump up and walk down the corridor with other children. Jean leaves me alone. My lunch tastes great.

Children who bully usually pick on others when adults aren't watching. It helps to stay close to teachers in places such as the dining hall and the school playground.

That afternoon, Mrs Simms finds me on the playground. **"Your mum called me,"** she says. **"Stevie, I didn't know you were being bullied. If it happens again, I want you to tell me straight away. You can leave early for lunch if you want to."**

Mr Jones, the headteacher, says children who have friends aren't bullied as much as children without friends.

I am learning how to make more friends.

Mum keeps an eye on me. She asks how I'm feeling and if I'm still being bullied. Mrs Simms says she is going to talk about bullying in lessons.

I'm glad I told my mum. I know I have adults and friends on my side. I don't let bullies like Jean bother me now.